New York/New York

masterworks of a street peddler

⟨DDD⟩

Far beneath
a steeplejack's solitude
another loner
discovers haunting views
everywhere
within the perimeters
of a harsh
subway-and-sidewalk world

New York/New York

masterworks of a street peddler

George Forss

presented by

David Douglas Duncan

Harvill Press

8 Grafton Street   London W1

1984

photography
George Forss

design-production-text
David Douglas Duncan

printing
Imprimeries Réunies
Lausanne, Switzerland

binding
Van Rijmenam
The Hague, Holland

publishers
McGraw-Hill Book Company
New York, N.Y., 10020

books by D.D.D.

This is War!-1951
The Private World of Pablo Picasso-1958
Treasures of The Kremlin-1960
Picasso's Picassos-1961
Yankee Nomad-1966
I Protest!-1968
Self-Portrait: USA-1969
War Without Heroes-1970
Prismatics-1972
Goodbye Picasso-1974
The Silent Studio-1976
Magic Worlds of Fantasy-1978
The Fragile Miracle of Martin Gray-1979
Viva Picasso-1980
The World of Allah-1982
New York / New York-1984

British Library Cataloguing in Publication Data
New York, New York. Forss, George
1. New York (N.Y.)—Description—1984
—Views
I. Title
974.7'1'043'0222   F128.37
ISBN 0-00-272553-3

Contents

Fleeting Images of a Great City

Saturday / summertime   Grand Central Station

Preface

He's a thief . . . that's heroic photography!

A street peddler's setup had nailed me in midstride. En route to Japan, I'd just telephoned my home in southern France from Grand Central Station before hurrying across town for lunch with old-time colleagues at *Life* magazine. I never got there. Astonishment, disbelief, excitement, confusion and admiration held me captive while my eyes swept the vendor's display of prints on a sidewalk between Madison and Park Avenues in midtown New York.

He must have stolen some of Ansel Adams' finest work . . . but Ansel never shot New York! So who's the photographer?

Almost every scene was a transfigured cliché of Manhattan. All of them were deluxe format and impeccably mounted. Some were masterpieces; the one beside my foot was incredible. Promises of romance and the mystery of lower Greenwich Village lurked in the evening gloom behind the World Trade Center whose twin pylons of industrial power still shimmered in an aurora of sunlight—modern cathedral spires painted with silver against the threatening sky. It seemed like El Greco's *View of Toledo* in the Metropolitan Museum, but updated—and yet there was still more. Magically, spanning the city, stretched across the entire width of the print, gleamed the elegance of Her Majesty, *Queen Elizabeth II*. Finally, four tiny craft were precisely and perfectly spaced alongside that enormous ship as she was being escorted down the Hudson River to the Atlantic Ocean, headed home.

I've never seen such a photograph . . . it will not happen again.

Stunned, I scanned the rest of the show. I didn't know any of the pictures or recognize the eye that created them. I was lost in a city I'd known for years but had never seen in this way before: Central Park abandoned under pristine snow; panoramic ghosts of skyscrapers glowing far beyond turbulent Fifth Avenue at dusk; the Battery veiled by seagulls and fog; spider webs of the Brooklyn-George Washington-Verrazano bridges ensnaring a dream-island city; the Empire State Building and stalagmite forests of steel-and-glass soaring into skies filled with sunbursts and spring clouds, or nothing but the purity of limitless space. They were the visions of a hermit-poet with a camera who created from reality a private mirage. Except for the portrait of a wistful black child there were no people anywhere in his exhibit, yet these photographs throbbed with the pulse of the city.

My glance was the fast in-depth search that every photographer learns on a battlefield. New Yorkers' faces sometimes resemble those seen in combat and often are nearly as challenging. This peddler was tough—six feet tall, burly, bearded, balding—really tough; probably a veteran pro-football linebacker now on hard times who had turned to an even more bruising, riskier trade. But something was wrong. His eyes didn't sweep the street looking for cops. I ignored the prints to watch him.

He was dressed for waiting in the concrete canyons where street grit cuts almost as cruelly as Gobi Desert sand. His prints were canted along a wall, braced against the biting winter wind. He moved and spoke without haste, secure in obvious self-assurance and an aloof but tragic serenity; a man whose gaze met other eyes with neither appeal nor antagonism. Squatting on the sidewalk—balanced easily on his toes—he talked quietly with passing clients, looking up, holding a couple of prints in massive but curiously pale hands. Then I saw his fingers with those nails richly walnut stained from years of submersion in photo developer. His eyes, blinking too often for a shaded November street, were red-rimmed, exhausted: he was a night printer selling in daylight.

Holy Christmas—he's the photographer!

While clumps of New Yorkers gathered before his street-gallery exhibit, I went through his work looking for flaws, searching for imperfections—dust spots, developer streaks, blocked shadows, hypo stains, burnt-out highlights—my eyes probing enlargement after enlargement, probably as carefully as his had the night before while making selections for the sidewalk. When I found more than one print of a subject, each matched the other to the slightest nuance of shading. All were of spectacular tonality, black-and-white, equal to the finest photographs by the giants of my time. I'd seen prints of the greatest, many of them friends for years. I'd also worked alongside some of the world's most meticulous darkroom technicians and printers who helped establish the reputations of several now legendary photographers of this century.

Then I read the crude, hand-lettered data sheet—almost scrawled, as though it was time wasted, a concession to the market place—where it was explained that the paper used for the prints was Kodak's newest emulsion, with promised, and hoped for, superior qualities. Two sizes were offered: 11 × 14 and 8 × 10 inches, all matt-mounted. There were also two combinations of prices: $5.90 for one 11 × 14, or $5.00 each if two were purchased. One 8 × 10 was $2.50; two cost $4.00. At the side of the price list I saw a peddler's license. On hands and knees, I read the name of the man who now stood at the far end of his display giving street instructions to a mother and her child, nothing in his hands:

George Forss, 729 East New York Avenue, Brooklyn 11203, New York

Not one print was signed.

Forss was rearranging something in his peddler's case when I pointed to *QE II* and *Central Park in the Snow*, and handled him my $10. We never exchanged a word. I couldn't! Tears of anger were in my eyes and probably would have drowned my voice. That morning, in one of life's curious twists of fate and timing, I'd read the *New York Times*, Section II, page one story about—of all people—Ansel Adams. One of his prints had been sold at auction for $22,000. The $5.00 *QE II* print now under my arm, signed or unsigned, was the equal of anything I'd ever seen by the master. And I felt that Ansel probably would have agreed.

That sidewalk purchase also reminded me of another day, in 1958, when I read that one of Pablo Picasso's 1905 portraits—the now-famed *La Belle Hollandaise*—had just been sold in a Sotheby's auction to an Australian museum for $250,000—at the time considered astronomical. Later that afternoon, while photographing him painting ceramics, I'd asked Picasso whether he remembered the picture. He looked at me for a moment, those luminous black-chestnut eyes amused either by my ignorance, thinking that he would have forgotten one of his paintings, or by the memory itself: "Yes, I remember. I was coming down to Paris from Montmartre with an armload of pictures, hoping to sell *something*. It began to rain. I went from door to door asking the shop-keepers' permission to leave my things for a few hours, protected from the storm. They threw me out. My pictures, too. I stood with them wrapped in old newspapers in a doorway until the rain stopped. Later that day I sold one for five gold francs, about twenty-five dollars today. It was *La Belle Hollandaise*."

This day, instead of going to *Life*'s offices, I headed for my hotel to get a camera (like most old professionals—except Henri Cartier-Bresson—I never carry a camera when not working) and almost ran back to where I'd just seen Forss. He and his pictures were gone.

That evening while looking again at Forss's prints I found a telephone number written in pencil on the back of each mounting board, black-on-black and nearly illegible. My anger of the morning welled up again, this time at Forss. Selling prints on the sidewalks of New York must be just about the most difficult and precarious way to earn a living in my profession. Modesty is appealing and admirable in artists, whether of minor inspiration or genius, but self-imposed anonymity—however idealistic —is a road that leads only to a commercial vacuum in photography. I dialed the number to Forss's world —to invite myself into what he probably treasured as sacred in an obviously antisocial life . . . his solitude. To discover such a paradox in a street peddler, especially in another photographer shooting New York City, elated me.

His phone kept ringing, yet I refused to hang up, sure that he was there, probably in his darkroom developing a print that couldn't be abandoned. Then a woman answered —twenty-five or thirty rings later. Breathless laughter. George couldn't come to the phone immediately, he was stuck in the photo lab. "I'm his mother—he's a good boy, isn't he?" I replied that I had no idea how good a boy he was, but as a photographer he was more than good—great! A torrent of words then surged over each other, almost flooding a telephone somewhere across the city.

"George is my oldest—I've had six. Another boy's a self-ordained street preacher. Lost one girl at eighteen, one's unmarried, another's a nurse. One boy has a terrible problem —drugs—can't get him in a hospital. I read cards. (laughter) I bet on Ronnie Reagan, knew he'd beat Jimmy Carter. Come have dinner. Italian—so am I . . . Norma. Can tell your future too. Couldn't read my own! (laughter) Married three times—bad luck with men, all hoodlums! A Swede, George's father—banks . . . deported—an Irishman and a German. (laughter) I taught George how to use a camera—I'm a photographer too. All he needs is a break. Here he is now."

His voice was flat—South Bronx flat . . . Brooklyn flat . . . combat foxhole flat . . . western deserts pioneer American flat . . . battered child of famine and war flat—no inflection, no emotion, no surprise, no haste, no suggestion of impatience at work disrupted, no curiosity about a stranger phoning in the night, no hint that life's roulette might change, and no betrayal of his aloneness. And yet, I felt that we each sensed the promise of comradeship in the other's voice.

"Mother was slow getting to the phone. She loved speaking with you. Talked a lot, for sure, like many handicapped older people." Handicapped? "Oh yes, and like most handicapped she tends to turn within herself. The phone's her escape. We heard you ringing. Couldn't stop my work. She had to walk across the room.

"She's a hunchback—head nearly touches the floor. Got arthritis. Says she's sorry keeping you waiting. Hopes you'll come to dinner sometime. Great cook—thinks she's a great photographer too. (dry chuckle) She was star-struck before the war. Orphan. Peddled newspapers around the nightclubs, belonged to a fan club. Bought a three-fifty camera, flash and all. Three dollars fifty. Then snapped celebrities—her stuff still looks pretty good." He probably said something else but I was numb, thinking of those crippled feet inching across a Brooklyn floor while I stubbornly kept the phone ringing, waiting for her son to answer.

George Forss's flat monotone cut through the night. I heard him calling to his mother, explaining that I was someone who'd bought a couple of pictures that day. I then told him I'd returned a few minutes later but he'd disappeared. "Yeah—the cops." But I'd seen his vendor's permit. "Don't mean a thing. Wrong side of the street—you stay too long in one spot—you snarl traffic—you're working too close to another peddler—anything. Must be in court tomorrow morning—lose half a day. Cost me sixty-five dollars—they even charge you for the truck that drags your stuff away. Sometimes they keep the prints. Guess somebody liked 'em, kinda nice even if they are cops following orders. Everybody on the sidewalk knows the rules. It's a game."

I told Forss that I wanted to buy more of his work the next day—where could we meet? The morning was out, he'd be in court. How about the same place where I first saw him, across from the Roosevelt Hotel, on Forty-fifth Street—about 1:30? He'd bring the shots he'd been printing when I phoned. Then I told him that I also was a photographer, named Duncan. "David Douglas Duncan?" Yes. "Duncan . . . heard you were coming apart. Won't tell you who told me. Glad you're not." He then said he'd try to be there a little earlier. He didn't eat lunch. For the first time that night I smiled: It was a typical comment of a Marine telling a buddy he'd heard he got zapped the day before, was "deeelighted" to see he hadn't—then both settling down to their C rations, a normal day's pleasantries finished.

The next day was warmer, winter's first chill had lost its grip on the city. I arrived ahead of time in order to watch Forss when he opened shop. I had a camera, and as he didn't know what I looked like, I could go about my business while he went about his. I'd been there only a moment when he appeared, also early, pushing his vendor's suitcase, coming from the subway under Grand Central Station.

If he remembered our conversation of the night before there was no evidence of it as he began leaning prints along his favorite wall. He never looked around for a photographer or anybody else. Customers began stopping even before his display was fully arranged, before he was satisfied with each picture's position—especially its degree of slant, making sure there was no surface glare. It was obvious he'd decided upon combinations the night before, attentive to interlocking relationships between different images. Some were clearly intended to be viewed—and bought—as pairs. Everything he touched revealed a critically tuned sense of composition and harmony. I guessed that his avocation—if he permitted himself one—was listening to classical music. I bought fourteen prints (for what it cost to fill the gas tank of my car in France) and introduced myself, which was rewarded with a nod and the steady gaze that met everyone on the sidewalk, then I headed for the Time-Life Building. As I walked away he called, "Mother and I welcomed your phoning."

Mr. Ray Cave
Managing Editor: *Time* Magazine
Rockefeller Center: New York 10020

Dear Ray: 21 November 1980

From that first moment when you responded to the photographs of street vendor George Forss, I've witnessed a staggering phenomenon—the entire Time-Life Building being turned on by an unknown man's work. Incredible!

First you, then Dmitri Kessel, Gjon Mili, Carl Mydans, Alfred Eisenstaedt; all of the photo lab (lab-chief George Karas asked immediately how to reach him to offer him a job); the travel department; the elevator guards; all of the super-brass (Chairman of the Board Andrew Heiskell, Editor-in-Chief Hedley Donovan, Henry R. Luce III, etc., who were gathered in the Board Room to screen a film on Eisie. Heiskell—"I'll pay him plenty more than five bucks for a *QE II* print." Hank Luce marked five for purchase.) Book Editor Steve Kanfer got his number from me and called him at home but learned he was back in court paying another fine—despite his vendor's license. Imagine! A talent like that fighting not only to survive in today's photo world —he has to battle the cops, too.

Ray, this is a Cinderella story. All of New York has walked right past his suitcase. Give him a picture essay. He's as great as Ansel Adams in many ways—and he's Everybody. He's ten million guys with a camera, shooting for the love of it. He's *happy* his prints sell for $5 . . . "everyone can buy them—*if* they like them."

This could be one of the great Christmas features of all time. A Japanese friend, at lunch yesterday (my printer for *Viva Picasso*), said: "You know, this is *my* New York—every foreigner's New York, because each picture was taken at the end of the subway, or on a ferryboat . . . the way we see it first."

That someone born in the South Bronx and from Brooklyn should still see it as a dream-city is a miracle.

This is Christmas!

Dave

Despite Ray Cave's instant enthusiasm for the story, and *Time* photography editor Arnold Drapkin's efforts to make plates immediately, newsbreaks of that period shattered all editorial timetables. Each week the Forss double-page feature was scheduled, momentous events forced it out of *Time*: President Reagan was shot, then the Pope. Hot-news events consume countless pages of weekly magazine space when civilization perishes a bit more, and low-key art stories like the one designed around George Forss are the first to disappear into the HOLD drawer in the layout room. I was in Japan periodically firing off prodding telexes to Cave and Drapkin. Answers came back promptly: "Love that sushi—Forss still our boy too—his story will run—sayonara."

And it did, seven months later, at the end of June 1981. George Forss never knew it, but Ray Cave and Arnold Drapkin gave him superstar treatment and *Time*'s red-carpet priorities at the engravers in Chicago. His two pages of pictures were printed in the most sumptuous duotone possible to reproduce on a weekly magazine's newsprint; equal to the way an Ansel Adams photo-essay (his lifetime's work) had been handled several years earlier, and used just one other time, for celebrations honoring the centennial of Pablo Picasso and his private world.

Everyone at Time-Life seemed to care about Forss: photographers, darkroom master-printers, editors, writers, researchers, art directors, copy readers and messengers and the top brass. Everybody was intrigued by his life and work—and rushed off trying to find him on the sidewalk before *Time*'s story broke and his prices skyrocketed. I'd returned from Tokyo and was again in New York the weekend Forss's pictures were finally on press and running—no catastrophe, anywhere, could bounce him again. I showed pre-publication photostats of the layout to Marilyn Sahner, promotion expert of the Time-Life empire. She phoned Tom Brokaw, across the street at NBC-TV. Forss was booked immediately on the "Today" show. His ship had come in . . . so it seemed.

I'd planned to fly home that night but Brokaw needed a backstop for his opening cut to Forss, so asked me to stay over to make a spot appearance during his introduction

—the program would be shot live a couple of days later. George arrived at dawn that morning with a dozen dramatic prints under his arm. Just before the cameras rolled, Jim Straka, the "Today" show's behind-the-lens studio floor-boss came over to ask what I was pitching, what was my latest book? We'd been friends for years, since I'd first shown war pictures on the program. When he saw Forss's shots going on the studio easels and heard a clipped sketch of his life, he just smiled and turned to his pals on the cameras saying, "Take a nap, Dave. Leave Forss to us."

That morning on the "Today" show, skyscrapers, bridges, tugboats, Fifth Avenue, Central Park, the Statue of Liberty, the World Trade Center, and the Empire State Building all floated in space, dissolved, then zoomed closer, only to fade and return in a parade of images blended together on the screen by a team of cameramen equally as tough as Forss, who loved *his* city because it was theirs, too. And Brokaw really knew what he had sitting beside him in the studio that morning as we all watched the monitor screens. There was no sound other than Forss's flat voice from the street riding over the photographs while an awakening nation listened.

When the cameras stopped and the lights dimmed, Tom Brokaw, movie critic Gene Shalit, weatherman Willard Scott, Jim Straka, and all the others on the set crowded around, asking to see his prints closeup—and to hold them for a moment in their hands. George lined everything up along one side of the studio, as on Forty-fifth Street. Shalit asked the price of a picture, wanting to buy it for his photographer son. Forss looked up and without blinking, said, "Ten dollars." Shalit's mustache and afro hair quivered. "Ten bucks! I just heard you tell the whole country that Dave bought them from you for five—didn't he, Tom?" Brokaw nodded, holding the *QE II* print in his hands. George Forss looked at them, eyes sharing his fun, and said, "Mr. Brokaw, *these* pictures are famous. They've all been on the 'Today' show."

I returned to France that evening, arriving home at noon the next day. As I walked in the door the phone was ringing—London calling, the British Broadcasting Company. A genial, Oxfordian voice came on the line introducing itself as that of a BBC-TV producer who'd seen the sidewalk-photographer program the day before during a stopover in New York. Where could they contact George? The BBC wanted to send a television unit to the States to film a half-hour program on Forss, his life and work, for worldwide distribution. George later told me that a five-man team came to Brooklyn and stayed a month or so. I kept waiting, but that's all he ever told me. I've never seen the film, yet have often wondered about that unlikely blend of Brooklyn and British voices weaving through the soundtrack of the program.

A year after meeting Forss, after seemingly continuous shuttle flights between France and Japan where a Picasso book had been on press, I was again in New York, exploring a vintage-automobile photobook idea with the press director of Daimler-Benz, North America. During a Chinese lunch, Leo Levine made his point fast and clear: "I'm trying to peddle *new* cars not old!" That "peddle" reopened my George Forss window looking onto the city. After a fast briefing, Leo suddenly envisioned a Mercedes gliding among Manhattan's monuments like never before, into back alleys and beside abandoned wharves, "really spooky places," where some of the world's most de luxe automobiles had never been photographed.

I found George at home. His mother had answered the phone, the same as the first time I called. The same flat "Hello, David"—he'd just come from court—"new judge, inflation, seventy-five dollars." No surprise, no questions, no shared secret plans . . . pure George Forss. I quickly explained that an immensely powerful European company might be able to use some of his camera technique in their advertising plans. He said he'd meet us within an hour, if possible—depended on the subway.

When Leo Levine saw that suitcase of prints (*QE II* is now framed in his living- room), it seemed that a new dimension of Forss's professional life would soon unfold. Mercedes would make all models of their cars available, anytime, for as long as George wanted to drive them around. "Pose 'em anywhere, George . . . just do for Mercedes what you've done to New York and the *QE II*." George Forss looked at Leo Levine for even longer than his customary pause before speaking, then replied: "Thank you for liking my work. But there's a problem. I've never had a car. I don't know how to drive."

George told me later that Leo arranged for a car and driver but they never got more than a few miles away from the Daimler-Benz headquarters in New Jersey, where the driver had a couple of beers while George made a couple of shots, which he showed me. They were dreadful—shots that wouldn't have sold cars to taxi-fleet owners in Bulgaria, where they will buy *any* Mercedes—which I told him. For the first time in our friendship, George really laughed: "That's what Leo said too." Then he caught the subway home. It seems that his vision was unrelated to the American, European, and Japanese four-wheeled dream. Camera in hand, he then returned to the sidewalks, to roam the streets of his city.

More recently, a book on the Moslem world kept me too involved with production timetables in Japan to be able to maintain contact with George and his world. I'd heard he was invited to lecture at the International Center of Photography on upper Fifth Avenue—probably speaking about selling prints on the sidewalk . . . several million light years away from the orbits of most photographers. He's still at home caring for his invalid mother, still printing at night, still working the sidewalk during the daytime, still paying for his peddler's license, and still paying fines in court. No museum has yet given him wall space, not one exhibit. But perhaps the sidewalk *is* his natural environment, his front page, his museum.

One of the highest tributes ever paid a photographer and his work was something I overheard while I photographed him on the street around the corner from Grand Central Station. Crowds poured toward the subways. Forss stood alone, like an enormous bear in a river with the torrent swirling around him shoulder-high, while he carefully erased finger smudges from a mounted print. Suddenly, a vast, middle-aged black lady broke free of the crush, approached him, and said: "Mister, I bought a picture from you last month. I've been looking for you ever since. Sorry, can't afford another one just yet. But my man told me to tell you that you are an *artist!*" Then she continued to the subway.

George Forss smiled, ever so faintly.

Perhaps this book should be titled *The George Forss Photographic Museum of New York*. But then no one would have understood, except those hurrying citizens of the city whose heart he seems to have captured . . . and an ever-widening circle of admirers who constantly ask: "Which is his street corner today?"

George Forss
of
The Bronx
and
Brooklyn

I try to live honestly
off the land
just beyond the edge
of
today's society

New York/New York

Lower Manhattan Island

Gulls welcoming Staten Island ferry

The Geometry of XXth-Century Man

Empire State Building / abandoned crane

Chrysler Building / United Nations Plaza

Radio City / Rockefeller Center

Sky Deck / Empire State Building ›

Shrines
of
the
Modern
American
Epoch

World Trade Center

Citicorp Center ›

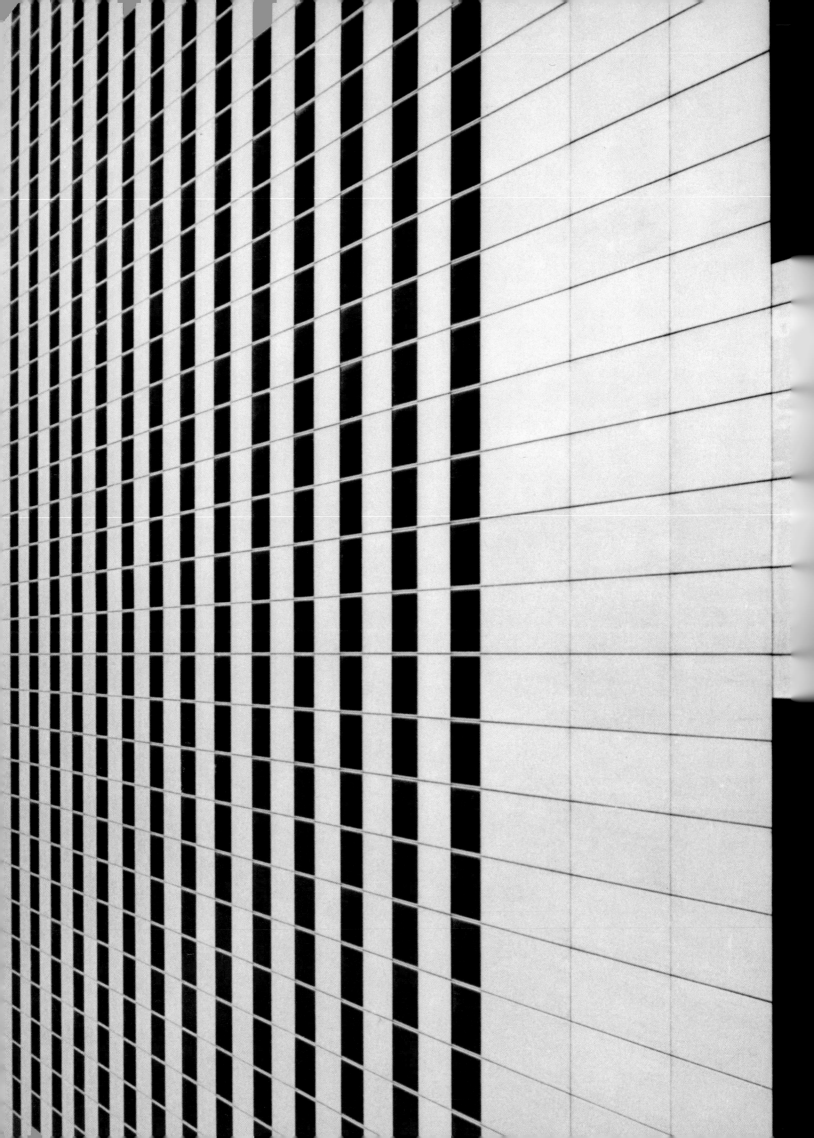

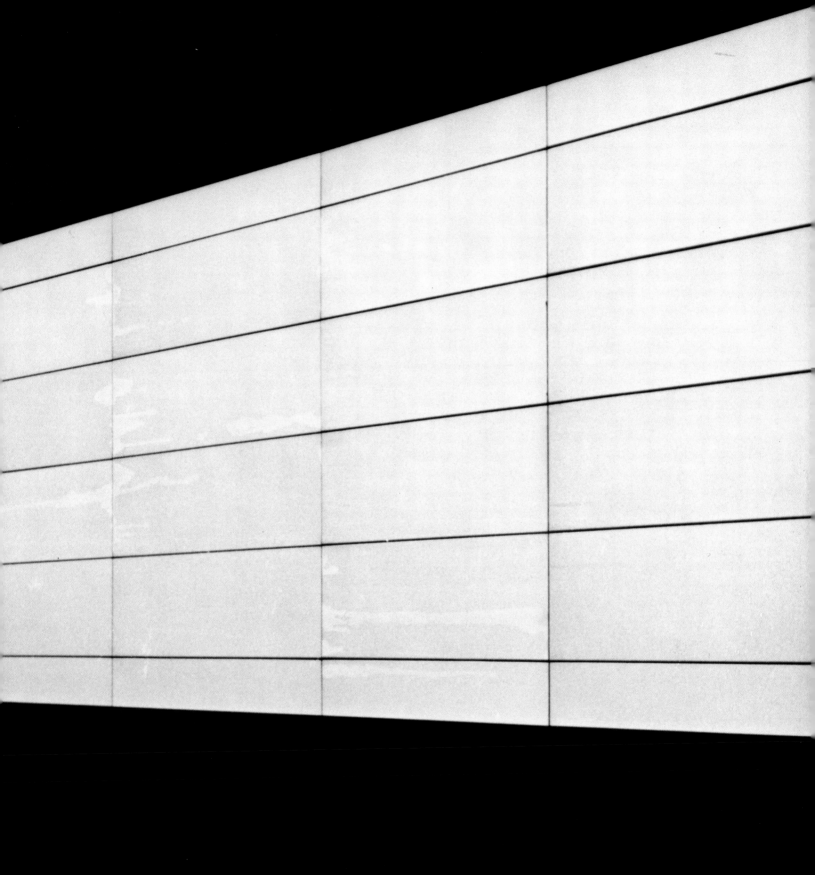

The
Bridge
to
Babylon

World Trade Center
Woolworth Building
Brooklyn Bridge
N.Y. Bell Telephone

Avenue of the Americas

Verrazano-
Straits
Bridge

Pan Am
Building
foyer

The Battery

Rush Hour
in a
Fairy-Tale
City

George Washington Bridge

Empire State Building

Nightly Exodus
of
Optimists and the Weary

Off-track bettors

Fifth Avenue/42nd Street ›

Twilight Mirage
of
An American Legend

Fifth Avenue / 59th Street

Autumn

Ghosts
of
Daumier's Lovers

by carriage
at sunrise through
Central Park

Uptown
from
a
Downtown Bus

Fifth Avenue / 57th Street

Kaleidoscope
of
Tomorrow and Yesterday

World Trade Center Mall

Avon Tower / Plaza Hotel
"Victory" ›
General Wm Tecumseh Sherman

East River / Upper Manhattan

East River/Lower Manhattan›

Winter

Frost Forest
on
Norma's Windowpane

57th Street / 7th Avenue

Williamsburg / Manhattan / Brooklyn bridges

Central Park / West 72nd Street ›

Rockefeller Center

Christmas tree lights and skaters

a
Tree
in
Brooklyn

Prospect Park

Norma's world

George's fantasy ›

April on Brooklyn Bridge

Yachting under the bridge ›

The Smell of Spring

escape for everyone,
almost everywhere...

May on Park Avenue
Seagrams Building Mall

Season-to-season
The Bronx Zoo ›

Summer

Dalena in Hemlock Forest
‹George's dream-bride

Washington Square
100° Fahrenheit

Birthday party

United States Bicentennial

Tune peddler / Chinatown

United Nations Plaza

Chrysler Building / East River regatta

Stockbrokers' messengers

26 WALL

Coffee break

Midtown Manhattan / Hudson River

Lovers' Rock / Weehawken, New Jersey

George Forss

sidewalk poet
with
a
camera

Manhattan from Bayonne, New Jersey

Self-portrait

RCA Building and George

Self-portrait

The
Dream-City
of
George Forss

Citicorp Center

The Diesel Pulse of Life Today

Brooklyn Bridge and Manhattan Island

Images ... Images ... Images

the
Future
and
Past

Visible Today

Street sculpture
River ruins
Ancestral graves ›

Terrifying first ride

Summer
at
Coney
Island

for
a
New
Generation
of
Americans

Merry-go-round

First
Snowfall

Central Park

Another New Year
in
The City of Lights

Norma's window
in
Brooklyn

Dedicated
to
The George Forss
Sidewalk Photographic Museum
of
New York City

Postscript

"Gimme that phone . . . gimme that BEAUTIFUL phone . . . you LUNATIC gimme . . . gimme . . . gimme . . . gimmeeeeee THAT PHONE! . . ."

The elderly bag-lady who had appeared from a telephone booth farther down the line in the Time-Life lobby stood shrieking at me—face contorted with rage—then turned and walked quietly out into the softest morning of springtime on Fiftieth Street. I apologized for the interruption, having called George early to arrange a meeting later in the day before I caught the plane back to France: I needed prints of his work to show book publishers in Europe.

His reply left me staring out across the street long after I had put down the receiver: "Don't worry, David—I know that voice."

There were other moments, during visits to New York, when I was shocked by my own ignorance of the forces that shaped such a man, who grew into adulthood within the welfare-society institutions of a suffocating, multiracial city. My own childhood was so different: pre-World War II Kansas City, Missouri—hunting, fishing, summer soda-pop stands and Boy Scout camp, all-white schools, $25 self-rebuilt jalopies, no cigarettes, no drinking, no broken homes, no more than a passing awareness of Hitler-Mussolini-Tojo in the outside world, loving a twice-devastated father who barely survived the Great Depression and who sat at the head of a dinner table where he and my mother never discussed their crushing financial troubles within earshot of the five children between them. Thus each time when the unexpected incident focused its harsh light on our unrelated lives, George's flat voice would explain: "David, perhaps you still don't understand. Our family is a bit different. My brothers and sisters were raised in orphanages and public homes where things are a little unusual. Please be patient . . . I'll try to do it (whatever "it" was at that moment) your way next time." When I replied that his way was okay with me, he almost smiled.

Like the time when I asked how things were at home and he said "Fine, except that Mickey set the place on fire when he burned his new blue jeans." Mickey? "Oh—Michael, my brother who's a few years younger and stays home all the time looking out the window. The cops and firemen were there and said, 'Okay, George, we'll let you take care of him again but watch out, 'cause next time the whole neighborhood may go up in smoke.' So we put out the blaze and Mother's okay . . . thank you for asking." Why burn blue jeans? "Oh . . . it's kind of hard for someone else to understand but I sold some prints last week and Mickey needed new pants so I got the blue jeans and gave them to him." Why the fire? "Yeah, I told you our family is somewhat different and I'm the one who has become sort of a success (chuckle) and so I bought Mickey the blue jeans since he couldn't buy them himself, so he burned them. But the firemen and cops are old friends like it always is in poor neighborhoods, and they let me take care of Mickey. We all aired out the house and Mickey's fine and is gentle and has no problems and loves us and that's really a nice way to be."

Norma, George's mother, and I have met only on the telephone: Manhattan-to-Brooklyn, Japan-to-Brooklyn, Switzerland-to-Brooklyn, Holland-to-Brooklyn, Saudi Arabia-to-Brooklyn and France-to-Brooklyn. We are the same age. After she heard of my desire to make a book of her son's photographs, she wrote me a 45-page letter in arthritic script, containing a hand-drawn good luck talisman and memories of her life.

"My childhood was spent in Greenwich Village among semi-literate, immigrant Italian-Americans like my mother. Many of our neighbors were alcoholics and wife-beaters —so was my father. My fantasies and ambition protected me. Besides becoming a photographer, I would have liked being a teacher or comedienne—I enjoyed helping others and making people laugh. But I also had a certain wisdom, common sense—I already felt that I would never fulfill myself, or find a place in society. I was superstitious, like my mother. I knew I had to settle for less. And my eagerness was too, too overwhelming. I married a Swede, an Irishman, a German—not *one*, but three hoodlum husbands!

"I was thirteen when I first started taking pictures. A cousin gave my brother an old camera to play with because it was broken. I asked if I could have it—took it to a pharmacist who fixed it. Nothing wrong but a loose lever. I loaded up, and from then on was snapping away. As far back as I can remember I had this tremendous urge to take pictures. We were very poor and film cost more than food. My mother forbade me to use the camera even though photography was one of my greatest joys. I was a dreamer, planning to become someone important, so I didn't let her or anyone else discourage me. I believe my mother tormented me because she loved me too much—she had lost her first two children. We were destitute. She did housework. My father was always out on a binge, was killed by train in '24.

"Broadway fascinated me. I loved music, singing, wrote many songs—to which my mother also objected. In '37 I started going to theaters, to see the stars backstage, telling my mother I was going to a movie. She passed away suddenly in '38—cancer. I felt lost but free. I joined the All Star Fan Club. Members took up a collection and I became their photographer. My new camera, flash and all, cost $3.55.

"I attended photography classes at a school in my neighborhood, learning to develop and print. A teacher liked my work. After my mother was gone I had to find a way to make money. I decided to peddle papers. This was before I met my first husband, Henry, George's father. After looking around for a good spot to sell, I decided on the Stork Club. I was chased away many times but kept going back. The doorman finally let me stay. He would give me half of his lunch sometimes. We were both Italians. I sold about twenty-four papers, got good tips, and made about ten dollars a night.

"One winter night I was crouched in an icy doorway when Mr. Walter Winchell came over to speak to me. He said 'Why aren't you home—aren't you cold?' And I replied 'Yes. But I'm selling papers.' So he bought a paper and gave me a quarter. Later on he mentioned me in his column, which read: 'New York is like this'—and somewhere in the middle he wrote 'the little newsgirl who peddles papers til 4 A.M. wears only socks in these temperatures. I guess she figures she'll get a closer look at the celebs.' The next night he asked if I saw the paper and I told him that I had and he said: 'Now you're famous!' But it wasn't true about me selling papers just to see the stars—I was trying to survive. Of course, the biggest stars visited the Stork Club—I got many good pictures. I would drop my papers, grab my camera, and snap. The doorman would yell at me —then share his wife's midnight sandwiches.

"I was never able to hang on to anything for very long. Children, dogs, a cat, even hoodlum husbands—everything I ever loved, or treasured, or felt pity for, was quickly taken away. Every time I had a child I'd say to myself I'm going to be both mother and father to my children. But I was cheated out of motherhood, for my children were taken from me. I never thought my children were a burden. I was capable of raising them. I never left them alone. When George was just a baby learning to walk—his father was up the river in prison for a two-year stretch—I always took him with me when I'd go out to buy films at Kodak. Even today, stricken with arthritis and twisted with pain when creeping to the window or door, I still feed the stray cats. How could I care for cats and not children! And I'm still full of ambition. I still have shining dreams. I make prints in George's darkroom, pictures I've never seen of my children, negatives taken thirty or forty years ago and put in a trunk because I couldn't afford to print them. Life forced me to push aside my work, my real love, photography. Like everyone, I came here unasked. I never understood the purpose of my being born. Was this the reason —taking pictures I never saw. Filling up welfare homes with my children, one by one, where they developed into adults without me?

"I taught George, my oldest, to take pictures. He had the same urge I did. My children learned to draw, write poems, compose songs—and we did live it up, even when I had to go begging door to door for the children. Had I listened to my mother, or others, I never would have reached my goal of being a photographer—nor would George. If I receive some recognition for my life, or for any creative work by my children, then, only then, will I believe that I was born for a purpose."

Once I asked George about his father—was he really a bank robber? "Well . . . a carpenter . . . odd jobs . . . one day I guess ambition—maybe problems at home—hit him real hard . . . started carving on a block of wood and ended up with a pistol . . . supermarkets . . . banks? Maybe a few. Mother's imagination, maybe . . . he was working his way up . . . a nice man . . . not sure where he is now."

Another day when he appeared to be blinking more than usual—eyes haggard and bloodshot from printing late into the night—I suggested that he take vitamin A and change his darkroom routine: print in the daytime and sell on the sidewalks around the theaters at night, the same way his mother sold her newspapers before the war.

"That's a good suggestion, David, but there's a problem. The garage next to our house . . . dead car batteries . . . especially in wintertime . . . everything on our block feeds off the same master power line. Whenever they turn on their battery charger my darkroom voltage drops then zooms all over the place—wrecks print after print. I work at night after they are closed then control every enlargement within fractions of a second . . . guess quality control will drive me crazy someday—or crazier. All my best lenses came from pawnshops—flawless glass sold by old-timers for peanuts. Those hockshop owners never knew what they had . . . happy selling them for nothing figuring they'd found a sucker and were unloading junk (chuckle). I've got some of the greatest gear in the world—some good ideas too . . . all I need is time."

There were moments when I fought sheer frustation and the temptation to treat him like any other professional photographer who shared my enthusiasms, problems, and experience—a grossly incorrect assumption. George instantly sensed my mounting irritation when all efforts to organize his work into a book seemed to explode in my face.

"David, I know I'm a problem. If no book actually appears, please understand— remember how much I appreciate your trouble in trying to work with me. It's always been my problem too . . . I've never followed anything to the end."

One weekend, I asked him to bring me all of his contact sheets so that I might start editing his New York shots—his photo-autobiography—through tough old professional eyes. George looked at me and said: "What contact sheets?" I explained, the contact sheets of those rolls of film he'd shot during his career as a photographer. "David . . . there aren't any." I still thought he'd misunderstood, or that I'd spoken too softly, or rapidly; so I repeated that I needed all of his contacts, where, thirty-five images to the sheet—every frame on a 35mm roll of film—I could search for those interrelated pictures which, when seen together, would constitute the first rough framework of his book.

He had never printed a contact sheet of his pictures in his life.

It was at that moment that I peered into the depths of the chasm separating the professional life of George Forss from every other photographer I had ever known. He took even longer in choosing the words of his explanation, than the afternoon several years earlier when he told Leo Levine of Daimler-Benz that he couldn't wheel the latest Mercedes dreamwagons around New York and photograph them . . . because he didn't know how to drive.

"David, I just shoot a roll of film . . . develop it . . . hold it up to the light . . . find the frame of the shot that I knew I could sell on the sidewalk when I took it. Then I go back into my darkroom—when the garage next door isn't charging batteries—and print it. The next day I catch the subway from Brooklyn to midtown Manhattan . . . find a good spot . . . and sell it. David . . . now I hope you will understand about no contact sheets . . . I'm just a peddler."

The next morning, shortly after sunrise, he brought me contacts of every roll of film he had ever shot in his life.

Photo Notes

For nearly one month after George printed all of his contact sheets, I sat alone at an uncluttered hotel table in Manhattan using only a reading lamp, photo-engraver's magnifying glass, and a red-wax pencil while pursuing one of the most elusive quarries of my life. I was trying to capture with his own negatives the throb of his heart; what he saw when he looked out through a window of that invisible prison cell that had been his home since childhood to gaze upon the profile of his beloved: New York/New York.

Even when seen through my eyes, the eyes of a veteran photo-journalist, the thread of George's life was so finely drawn, and surfaced so infrequently, that I often lost my way when it became nearly invisible as it meandered among all of his other photographs that covered my table. Much of *any* photographer's work is debris (flotsam cast up daily, as on the beach near a great city), to be pushed aside but never discarded, since it may be viewed in another context later when it adds the missing verb, or noun, or adjective to something that was a visual statement earlier—but no one understood. Not even the photographer with the greatest imagination and vision.

Many long days were spent excavating among his contact sheets, devoting more patience and energy and concentrated attention to his work than I ever did as an archaeology student at the University of Arizona searching for pre-Columbian pot shards and arrowheads. Most of his panoramic shots of New York were so pure technically that I did little more than marvel at his craftsmanship and mark them for straight enlargement. And I was moved almost to awe by his ability to convey the impression of a crossroads of humanity, without showing a single person. His mother's restricted-to-one-room existence as an invalid was revealed in the beauty of the morning frost of her breath on her winter windowpane (they had no heat many days), instead of focusing on her freezing, arthritic misery. In fact, among all of the pictures by this man who had moved his stricken mother out of their old brick home in the Bronx after arsonists tried to burn it to rubble, there was not one shot of protest or whining complaint about his life, and luck. Rather, it seemed that his photographs revealed an unending effort to enshrine his dream-city on a pedestal of love.

Norma's window was seen again in springtime when raindrops pearled the glass behind a newly leafed plant on the sill; and the same window still again, late in the year—the plant shriveled and dead—with Norma's golden-eyed black cat perched next to the glass while staring down into the narrow alley beneath her room where, even there, she no longer can walk.

Some of his most provocative photographs were single-frame multiexposures, surrounded by scenes of the city, where I found that he had broken his own proscription —exorcising people from his work. Or so I interpreted his camera code after looking at thousands of his pictures. For whatever reason—fantasy, challenge, timidity, but never accidental good luck—he fired once, fast, to capture his primary target, then rewound the shutter to fire again, adding a secondary and usually completely different but relevant subject and dimension to the picture. Young ice skaters of Rockefeller Center, a wraithlike Chinese girl flutist, toughened-by-disappointment off-track bettors heading home, Wall Street messengers sunbathing during their lunch hour, his friend Dalena (triple exposure!) as a turn-of-the-century bride, and his ethereal architectural dream of New York.

The man, himself, appeared to possess no vanity. I found a roll of film taken among the Hudson River wastelands and collapsing wharves (Leo Levine would have loved the place as counterpoint backgrounds for his Mercedes thunderbolts) in the center of which there were two frames showing a stripped-down racing bicycle draped with an old army canteen, picnic basket, and a camera bag. The next shot was of George in his work pants and undershirt slouched on a rocky point overlooking the river—like a taxicab driver resting after changing a flat tire. In crystalline afternoon light across the river, from the Statue of Liberty to the Brooklyn Bridge suspended on its steel cobwebs, lay the heart of New York—placed with surgical refinement under his unshaven chin. A self-portrait! There was only one negative, not duplicated in the event he miscalculated the angle, the camera shutter misfired, or the film got scratched later. No thought given to shooting another frame. The photograph, of course, was taken on a tripod with his camera set at automatic exposure which allowed between 8-and-15 seconds for pressing the shutter, running to his preselected posing location, then waiting for the click.

It was the work of a master: a photograph visualized and executed entirely in the mind of the artist, who had planned every aspect of the composition to within a fraction of a millimeter, then fulfilled his dream-of-the-moment without permitting his own self-image to interfere. When I found that frame—George told me later that it never had been printed ("Nobody on the sidewalk would ever buy *that!*")—I felt the same as the day when I first saw his exhibit on Forty-fifth Street and stopped in wonderment— mystified by the touch of an artist whose name I did not know.

Photo Data

"It's horrible . . . *horrible!* Alfred Eisenstaedt gingerly removed his glasses and peered at me through eyes slowly recovering from a cataract operation, my dummy copy of *New York/New York* on a table of his hideaway office in the Time-Life Building. I was dumbfounded by his sledgehammer criticism—he knew how long I'd been working to shape George Forss's photographs into a book. This was another Eisie, not my friend of nearly forty years. I just stared at him in disbelief while he finished polishing his glasses, put them on again, and refocused on my face.

"Oh . . . my *God!* David, I didn't mean the book! I meant my needing *two different* pairs of glasses. Look at me! Every time I move, reach for a camera, try to read, look at a painting, find a record—anything . . . glasses . . . glasses . . . *glasses!* It's *HORRIBLE!* But do me a personal favor. May I take a picture of George and you for the book jacket?" Then he laughed softly to himself, and said: "Maybe, if my shot is good enough, he'll explain how he took those incredible multiple exposures." I told him I'd been wondering about the same pictures, and so had many of our old *Life* colleagues.

Because so much of the technology of photography is something of a bore, really (lenses, cameras, films, chemicals-on-paper and fraction-of-a-second exposures—the nuts-and-bolts of a craft which, in special hands or with a magic touch of luck, may ascend to the level of art but who can imagine Picasso, or Braque, telling the other what brush, paint, or canvas he was using while they were creating Cubism); and because Henri Cartier-Bresson wrapped up the essence of great photography in three words when he remarked that it all boils down to "the decisive moment" and then returned to illustrating what he meant, such tedious shop talk never entered my conversations with Forss during the nearly four years that this book was evolving through an extraordinarily convoluted gestation period before emerging as *New York/New York.*

However, with book publication nearing reality (which George did not yet fully believe . . . and Norma dreaded: "Now, I'm waiting for the *bad* news!"), the day arrived when I had to confront these final pages and the fact that it would have been a failure of curiosity and professionalism had I not asked him to decode some of his multiple exposures, secrets I couldn't crack by myself. His answers came back immediately over the telephone—cryptic, clear, cosmic; ranging across the full spectrum of lens optics, camera engineering, filter properties, developer controls and chemistry, film characteristics, enlarging factors, light-and-shadow ratios, personal disciplines . . . and private dreams.

Here is what I learned: Bon Voyage to anyone sailing off to navigate the same ocean.

Page 46: George Washington Bridge at sunset and Hudson River Drive 45 minutes later. Double exposure. Plus-X film. Exakta 35mm camera. Schneider Isco-Westron 35mm F 2.8 lens. First exposure of bridge at 7:30 P.M., camera clamped to TV mast; F 16 at 1/8 second. Second exposure for Hudson River Drive, at 8:45 P.M.; F 16 at 13 seconds: both first and second exposures controlled by using lens cap while shutter remained open for 75 minutes.

Pages 56-57: Uptown from a downtown bus. Double exposure. Hand-held (while delivery messenger riding bus). Plus-X film. Exakta 35mm camera. Schneider Westanar 50mm F 2.8 lens. Both exposures F 4 at 1/50 second. First exposure shooting west on 57th Street. Shutter rewound without advancing film. Second exposure; focus on raindrops splattering bus window.

Page 59: Kaleidoscope of a pageant city. Avon Building, Hotel Plaza, "Victory" statue and General William Tecumseh Sherman (between 57th and 59th streets on Fifth Avenue). Double exposure. Plus-X. Rapid Omega 6 × 7cm camera. Schneider Xenotar 80mm F 2.8 lens. Both exposures F 11 at 1/250 second. Yellow-green filter. First shot: camera aimed northwest at statue. Shutter rewound. Forss then walked across 59th Street into Pulitzer Square, aimed camera southwest to include Avon Building and Hotel Plaza (following a tiny wax-pencil dot on viewfinder marking tip of fingers of "Victory" which he aligned with edge of Avon Building) and fired. As usual, there is only one negative. He went on to his next subject and idea—without backstop protection in the event this idea didn't work. He lives and works in a world far removed from the motordrive photographers of today, whose films of endlessy repeated shots of the same slightly varied subject are choking photo labs around the world.

Pages 70-71: Rockefeller Center skating rink. Double exposure. Plus-X film. Alpa 9 35mm camera. Angenieux 135mm F 3.5 lens. Both exposures F 5.6 at 1/250 second. First shot of sculpture. Shutter rewound. Long, selective waiting for precisely placed skaters —based on memory of sculpture position for first image—then shot second exposure.

Pages 84-85: George's dream-bride; Hemlock Forest, Bronx Botanical Gardens. Triple exposure. Plus-X film. Galvin 6 × 7cm view camera with roll-film back. Berlin Doppel Dagor 90mm F 6.8 lens. Total exposure: F 45 for 40 seconds. First exposure (farthest image): 20 seconds. Second exposure (center image): 14 seconds. Third exposure (nearest image): 6 seconds. Dalena, George's friend, is an actress, poet, dancer, and mime capable of holding each predetermined position perfectly (she choreographed her own poses, adding the slightest motion for esthetic reasons to the center image). Lens cap used to control total time-exposure. Camera, of course, on tripod.

Pages 88-89: Tune peddler in Chinatown, and Robert Abrams bilingual political-campaign banners strung between buildings overhead. Double exposure. Plus-X film. Exakta 35mm camera. Schneider Isco-Westron 35mm F 2.8 lens. First exposure: shot from street corner as girl played "bitonal tune" (chuckle) in front of drugstore; F 4.5 at 1/30 second. Shutter rewound. Second exposure: Forss stepped into center of street and shot into sky at 45-degree angle, to place girl within context of the political moment and juxtapose the languages of the Chinese-American neighborhood—while fulfilling his own artistic desires. This is a classic example of a photograph that was "made," not "taken." As revealed, again, in the following picture made on Wall Street, it is this quality of cerebral and artistic fulfillment that lifts some of Forss's photographs to the highest levels of our profession; augmented by fanatical darkroom disciplines.

Pages 92-93: Wall Street. Double exposure. Plus-X film. Alpa 9 35mm camera. Angenieux 90mm F 1.8 lens. First exposure: shot across Wall Street at façade of building where messengers were enjoying coffee break and lunch hour; F 4 at 1/250 second. Shutter rewound. Changed lenses. Schneider Isco-Westron 35mm F 2.8 lens. Second exposure: without changing his position, Forss fired straight overhead at overhanging buildings and American flags; F 11 at 1/100 second. Yellow-green filter.

Pages 100-101: RCA Building and George Forss self-portrait. Triple exposure. Plus-X film. Exakta 35mm camera. Schneider Westanar 50mm F 2.8. All three exposures: F 5.6 at 1/50 second. First exposure: the wall surrounding sunken pavilion (restaurant in summer, ice skating rink in winter). Second and third exposures: camera aimed at now-gone reflection pool under the sculpture suspended on west wall of pavilion to shoot reflection of RCA tower, his reflection, and that of the Associated Press Building. It is difficult to detect that the two images of him are different, until one studies his hands and their relation to his shoulders and the wall.

Pages 102-103: Citicorp Center. Triple exposure. Plus-X film. Exakta 35mm camera. Schneider Isco-Westron 35mm F 2.8 lens. Waist-level groundglass focusing device. Each of the three exposures: F 11 at 1/500 second. Yellow-green filter. Photo-cubism by George Forss. While writing the text and captions for this book, I tried to imagine those pictures George might have made had he been as free as my other photographer friends, or myself—had he not been forced to put aside his cameras while confronting almost paralyzing responsibilities at home. Still, working without help from anyone, he has produced images of New York that I find to be more creative, profound, and rewarding than those of any photographer (with the exception of Ernst Haas) whom I know, or whose prints I have seen—including the now legendary icon Alfred Stieglitz, and his views of the city.

Page 110: McGraw-Hill Mall, Sunday afternoon, 5 February 1984. Snow, rain, low fog. Triple exposure; two of them hand-held. Plus-X film. Exakta 35mm camera. Schneider Isco-Westron 35mm F 2.8 lens. First exposure: miniature tripod; map of world hemispheres in bronze on floor of patio; F 4.5 at 1/15 second. Shutter rewound without advancing film. Second and third exposures, hand-held; of chrome-steel sculpture and tops of skyscrapers in snow and fog; F 6.3 at 1/50 second.

After seeing Forss's work, Douglas Kirkland—an old friend from *Look* magazine who later moved to Hollywood—slowly shook his head, then carefully handed back the prints: "Now, it's a better morning . . . and what lessons we all can learn from this man of the streets."

Perhaps a fragment of George's itinerant life as a sidewalk poet with a camera was revealed by an anecdote he told me about his conventionally photographed (but monumental) print of *Queen Elizabeth II* and the World Trade Center. Before leaving Brooklyn, he reconfirmed the sailing hour of the Cunard Line's superstar; normally about 7:45 P.M. during July. He rode his bike to Jersey City, found a perfect position on a pier (later burned to the water), where he set up his tripod and Alpa 9 35mm camera, loaded with Plus-X film. Then he waited—and waited. The sun sank almost to the horizon. It was heartbreaking, because the clouds over New York were unreal —with a storm behind the city—a photographer's dream-backdrop. He checked and constantly adjusted his lens: Schneider Xenon 50mm F 1.8, set at F 8 with a yellow-green filter. Shutter speed: 1/250 second. But it was a lost sidewalk best-seller—a wasted day. He'd picked up his camera and tripod to leave, when Spanish-speaking children, fishing nearby, began waving and shouting: "Sheep's coming! . . . sheep's coming!"

Today, George Forss smiles—almost laughs—when recalling the incident. "I must have looked like a human pinwheel . . . nothing but arms and legs—like all four of the Marx brothers *and* Charlie Chaplin combined, trying to get my camera back to its place. And I even kicked the tripod while shooting!" . . . with a last blaze of sunlight spotlighting the regal lady as she moved silently across the greatest stage in the world.

It being a pleasant summer evening, he then rode his bicycle up along the Hudson River to George Washington Bridge, down Broadway through Manhattan Island and across Brooklyn Bridge—just sightseeing around his city for all of the twenty-three miles until he finally arrived home, after midnight. Norma was waiting for him with his dinner.